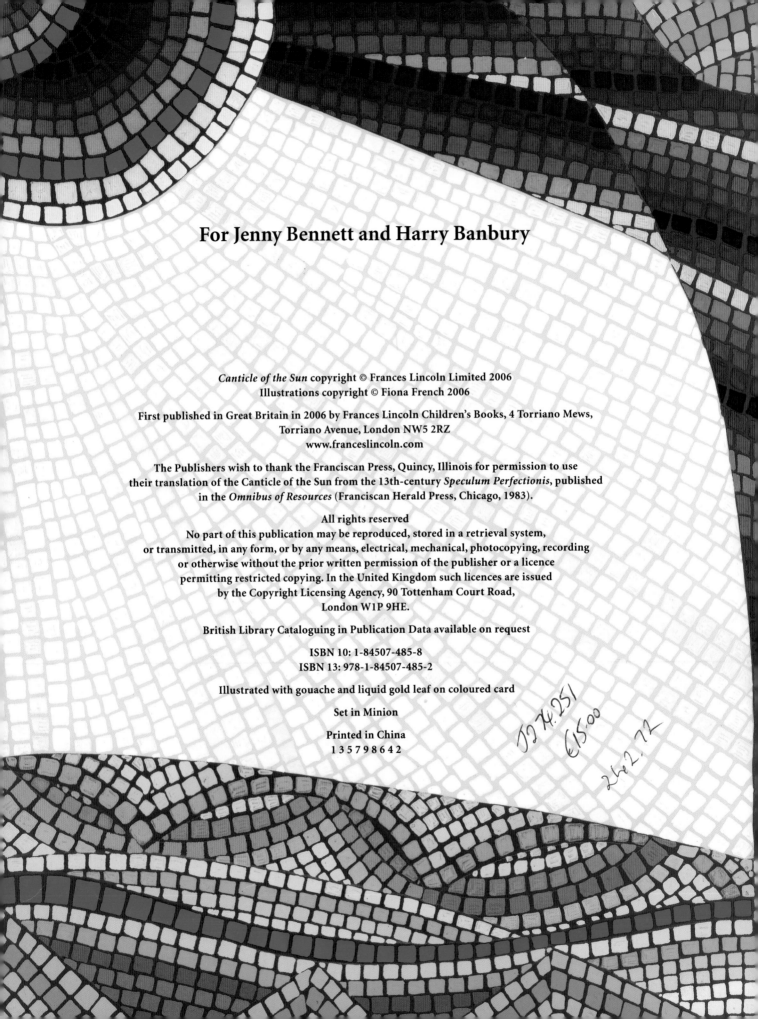

For Jenny Bennett and Harry Banbury

First published in Great Britain in 2006 by Frances Lincoln Children's Books, 4 Torriano Mews,
Torriano Avenue, London NW5 2RZ
www.franceslincoln.com

The Publishers wish to thank the Franciscan Press, Quincy, Illinois for permission to use
their translation of the Canticle of the Sun from the 13th-century *Speculum Perfectionis*, published
in the *Omnibus of Resources* (Franciscan Herald Press, Chicago, 1983).

British Library Cataloguing in Publication Data available on request

ISBN 10: 1-84507-485-8
ISBN 13: 978-1-84507-485-2

Illustrated with gouache and liquid gold leaf on coloured card

Set in Minion

Printed in China
1 3 5 7 9 8 6 4 2

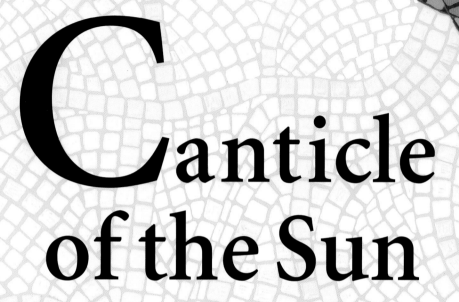

Canticle of the Sun

A Hymn of Saint Francis of Assisi
Illustrated by Fiona French

F

FRANCES LINCOLN
CHILDREN'S BOOKS

Most High, Almighty, good Lord,
thine be the praise, the glory, the honour,
and all blessing.

To thee alone, Most High, are they due
and no man is worthy
to speak thy name.

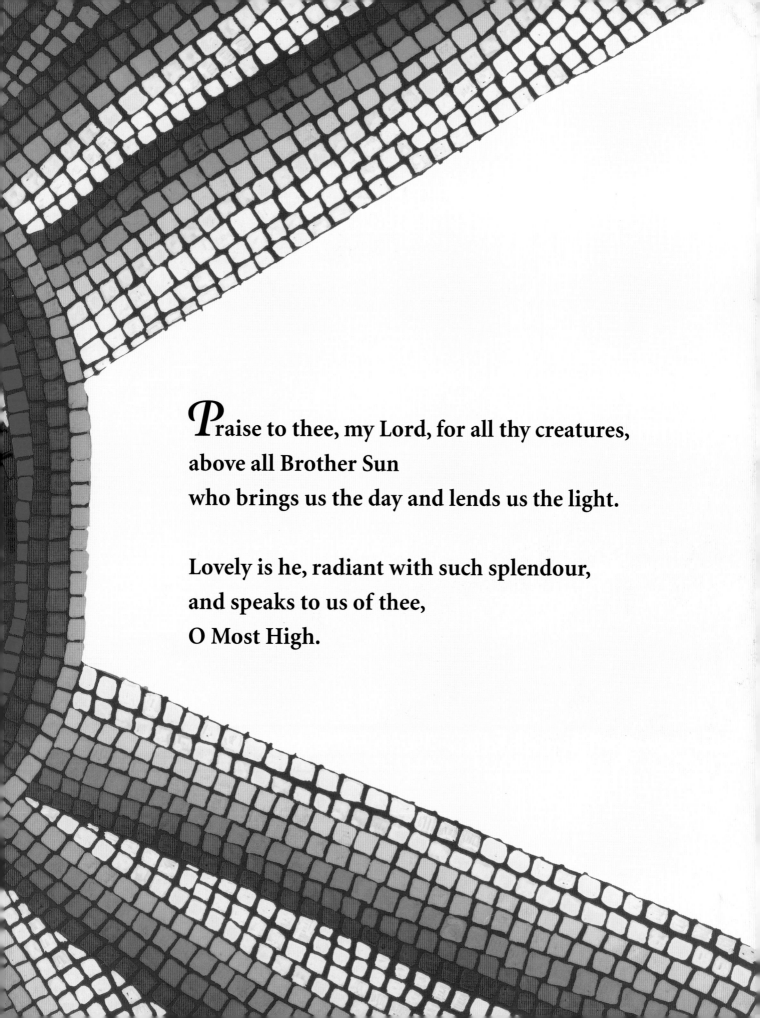

*P*raise to thee, my Lord, for all thy creatures,
above all Brother Sun
who brings us the day and lends us the light.

Lovely is he, radiant with such splendour,
and speaks to us of thee,
O Most High.

*P*raise to thee, my Lord,
for Sister Moon and the stars
which thou hast set in the heavens,
clear, precious, and fair.

*P*raise to thee, my Lord, for Brother Wind,
for air and cloud, for calm and all weather,
by which thou supportest life in all
thy creatures.

Praise to thee, my Lord, for Sister Water,
who is so useful and humble,
precious and pure.

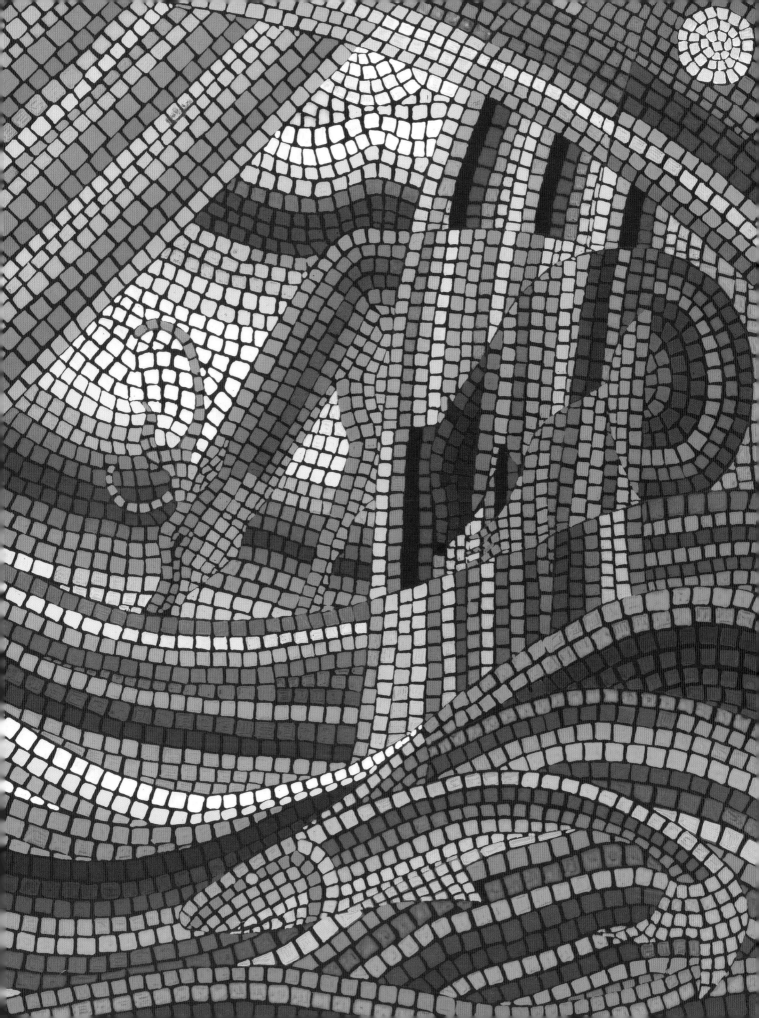

*P*raise to thee, my Lord, for Brother Fire,
by whom thou lightest the night;
he is lovely and pleasant; mighty and strong.

Praise to thee, my Lord, for our sister Mother Earth
who sustains and directs us,
and brings forth varied fruits, and coloured flowers, and plants.

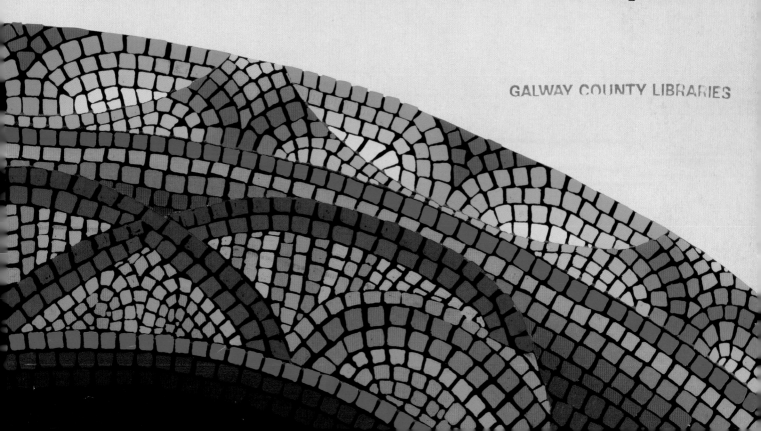

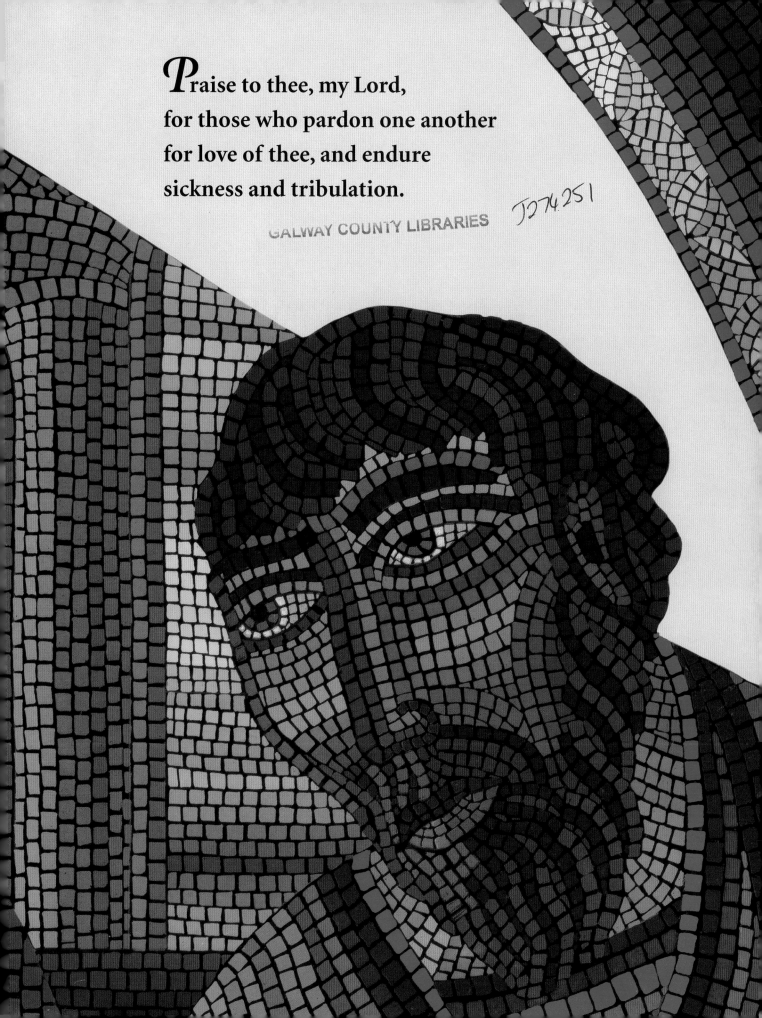

Praise to thee, my Lord,
for those who pardon one another
for love of thee, and endure
sickness and tribulation.

Blessed are they who shall endure it in peace,
for they shall be crowned by thee,
O Most High.

*P*raise to thee, my Lord, for our Sister Bodily Death
From whom no man living may escape:
Woe to those who die in mortal sin.

Blessed are they who are found in thy most holy will,
for the second death cannot harm them.

*P*raise and bless my Lord.
Thank him and serve him
with great humility.

Saint Francis of Assisi

Saint Francis is often described as 'the little poor man of Assisi'. Born Francesco Bernadone in 1181/2, the son of a well-to-do cloth merchant, he was a lively young man who dreamed of military glory, but he abandoned his worldly ambitions at the age of 19 while a prisoner-of-war in Perugia. He started to experience visions of Christ and Mary, and in 1210 he founded an order of friars known as the Franciscans, who took a vow of poverty. His rejection of the Church's worldliness, his love of nature and his humble, unassuming character earned him an enormous following throughout Europe. He was the first known Christian to receive the *stigmata*, spontaneously appearing wounds in his hands, feet and side similar to the wounds borne by Jesus Christ on the cross. These caused Francis great suffering, but he kept them a secret for many years so as not to draw attention to himself.

Music and prayers were such a part of Francis' life that he often gave voice to his feelings in writing and song. His most famous work, the *Canticle of the Sun*, shows his closeness to the wonders of creation as he embraces them one by one, calling them 'brother' and 'sister'. The final part of the canticle, in praise of Brother Death, was written just before Francis' own death in 1226. He was canonised in 1228.